# TRACEY TURNER
Illustrated by Sally Kindberg

# HOW TO make a HUMAN out of SOUP

## LITTLE, BROWN BOOKS FOR YOUNG READERS
lbkids.co.uk

LITTLE, BROWN BOOKS FOR YOUNG READERS

First published in Great Britain in 2015 by Hodder and Stoughton

1 3 5 7 9 10 8 6 4 2

Text copyright Tracey Turner, 2015
Illustrations copyright Sally Kindberg, 2015

The moral rights of the author and illustrator have been asserted.

A CIP catalogue record for this book
is available from the British Library.

ISBN 9780349124131

Printed and bound in Great Britain by
Clays Ltd, St Ives plc

The paper and board used in this book are
made from wood from responsible sources.

Little, Brown Books for Young Readers
An imprint of
Hachette Children's Group
Part of Hodder & Stoughton
Carmelite House
50 Victoria Embankment
London EC4Y 0DZ

An Hachette UK Company
www.hachette.co.uk

www.hachettechildrens.co.uk

*For Toby (of course)*
*and all the children and staff*
*at Widcombe Junior School.*

# Author's note

There's a timeline on pages 115-119 so you can keep track of when things were evolving, dying out, exploding, etc. Tricky words are explained on pages 121-125.

# CONTENTS

# 1
# Human Soup

Prepare to boggle your mind as we try to answer some of the most important and amazing questions ever asked . . .

Bring a packed lunch, and don't forget your time machine because we'll be doing a fair bit of time-travelling.

Some protective clothing might be a good idea, too, to cope with all the exploding volcanoes and meteorites and things.

We'll be examining green slime (for a few billion years), popping in on the dinosaurs, meeting some of the strangest animals that ever lived, and saying hello to some close relatives you never knew you had.

But first, let's take a look at the most important recipe in the history of the world . . .

# Recipe for HUMAN SOUP

Around 4.6 billion years ago, the surface of the Earth was a super-hot primordial soup, with nothing living in it. Now there are jellyfish, hamsters, cabbages . . . and people. So, how do you make a human out of soup?

*How on Earth did that happen?*

*PSSHT*

## INGREDIENTS

- Water
- Silica
- Mixed gases
- Selection of amino acids
- Assorted minerals
- Large pinch of salts

*ooh*

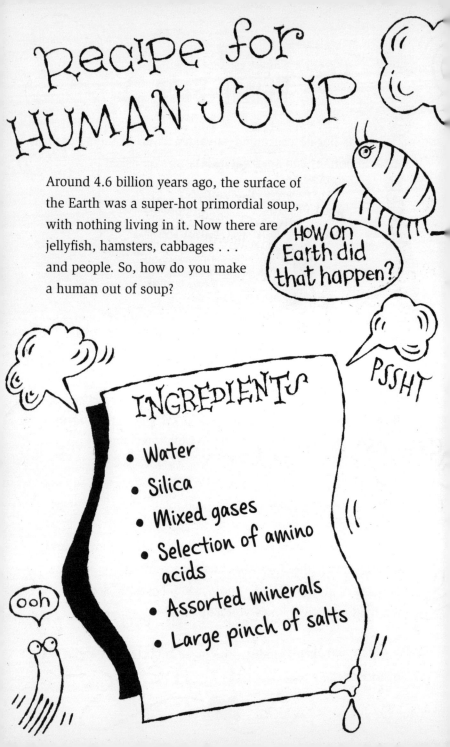

# In the Beginning . . .

Planet Earth was formed from bits and pieces whizzing around the sun 4,600 million years ago. At first, it was frazzle-to-a-crisp-in-an-instant scorching hot. After about 600 million years, Earth had cooled down a bit. Even though there wasn't any life, things were quite exciting: volcanoes were erupting, massive storms were raging, meteorites were smashing into the Earth, and the primordial soup was fizzing and blipping and turning into new molecules.

## ATOMS AND MOLECULES

Everything is made of atoms – you, this book, the stars, everything. They're like amazingly titchy building blocks, and there are lots of different kinds. (In fact almost all of them were made inside exploding stars – but that's another story.)

A molecule is a group of two or more atoms that stick together to make different things – for example, water molecules are stuck-together hydrogen and oxygen atoms.

## What You Have in Common with a Goldfish

Bubbling away in the primordial soup were minerals, which made the Earth's rocky crust, and water, which made it soupy.

There were also amino acids, which are molecules made mainly of hydrogen, oxygen, carbon and nitrogen. Over time – a very long time, and maybe with the help of bolts of lightning and volcanic eruptions to get things moving – the amino acids formed ribonucleic acid. This is usually shortened to RNA.

The RNA was a molecule with a special ability: it could copy itself. Over time, RNA got better and better at copying itself. Then it evolved an outer casing for protection. You have to imagine some very dramatic background music here, because . . .

# LIFE ON EARTH HAD BEGUN!

Eventually, an even cleverer self-copying molecule evolved, with an even more difficult name. It's called deoxyribonucleic acid, but happily we can just say DNA for short. It's the basis of all life on Earth, and it's what you have in common with a grizzly bear, a pineapple and a goldfish.

Really?

Obviously, a lot had to happen for the DNA to make human beings and fish and things, and that's what this book is all about.

But hang on a minute. How does anyone know about RNA and DNA? After all, there was no one around to see it.

Well . . . the truth is that no one knows for sure, but most scientists agree with this version of events, based on studies of the living things that are around today, as well as ancient fossils. There are different theories, though.

Right now, a scientist somewhere is trying to recreate conditions on Earth billions of years ago to show how life emerged from the primordial soup. Maybe some day one of them will prove how it happened. But until then we don't really know, and scientists will carry on arguing and trying to work it out.

Before we take a closer look at the very first life on Earth, and find out how utterly thrilling it was, let's fast-forward several thousand million years. We're off to the nineteenth century, by which time all sorts of different life forms had turned up. Some of them were human beings, who'd started to wonder about the rest of life on Earth, and how it had got there.

# 2

# Darwin and Wallace's Dazzling Discoveries

Until the 1800s, most people explained the amazing variety of creatures that share the planet with us as the work of God (of one kind or another). But some people thought there might be a bit more to it than that.

## The Age of the Earth

How long ago do you think life on Earth began? (There's a clue on page 4.) Is it . . .

a)    **Thousands of millions of years ago?**

b)    **Sunday 23 October, 4004 BC?**

I'm guessing you answered a), but Archbishop Ussher, who lived in the 1600s, spent ages working out that answer b) was when God created the first living things – a man and a woman called Adam and Eve. He didn't know that the first cities and empires had already existed long before that, and he took what it said in the Bible very seriously indeed. So did lots of other people, but not everyone agreed with Ussher.

In fact some people thought he was spouting utter nonsense. They believed:

- that life had existed on Earth for a really long time (millions, not thousands of years)

- that it had begun with one living thing which is the common ancestor of everything else

- that living things had changed over time, and that some creatures had become extinct.

But no one had a really convincing theory about it until Charles Darwin and Alfred Russel Wallace came along in the 1800s. They would probably have made Archbishop Ussher foam at the mouth, if he hadn't died in 1656.

# Voyages of Discovery

I hope you've packed your swimming kit, because we're off to some beautiful tropical islands teeming with wildlife. On some of them live huge orange-haired apes and birds of paradise. On others there are absolutely enormous tortoises and all sorts of other weird creatures.

These islands are halfway around the world from one another – the Galapagos Islands, and the islands of Malaysia and Indonesia. They're where Charles Darwin and Alfred Russel Wallace came up with their theories about how living things have changed over time, from the very first life on Earth into all the different kinds of plants and animals we can see today.

Charles Darwin's the name. I looked at giant tortoises on the Galapagos Islands, 960 km from the coast of Ecuador in South America.

Galapagos Islands

Hello, I'm Alfred Wallace. I travelled to the Malay Archipelago where I collected nearly 126,000 specimens. Over 5,000 of them were completely new to science!

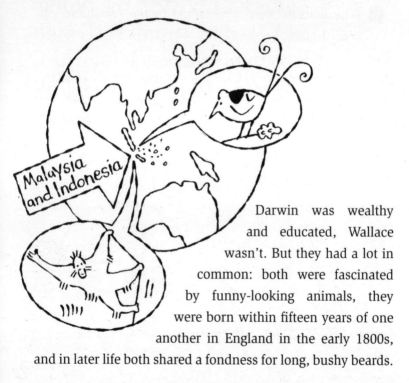

Malaysia and Indonesia

Darwin was wealthy and educated, Wallace wasn't. But they had a lot in common: both were fascinated by funny-looking animals, they were born within fifteen years of one another in England in the early 1800s, and in later life both shared a fondness for long, bushy beards.

Darwin set off on a round-the-world journey as a ship's scientist. Wallace made a living by collecting specimens for museums – this often meant shooting them and shipping them back to Britain, which tended to be how the Victorians studied animals – and this took him all over the world, too.

They noticed similar things about the islands they visited:

- Some of the creatures that lived there were unlike animals that lived anywhere else in the world.

- The animals were well suited to the conditions on their islands.

They made observations, asked questions, scratched their beards, and came up with very similar theories about life on Earth. They realised that living things that aren't found anywhere else can evolve on remote islands because they're cut off from the rest of the world. For example, the giant tortoises Darwin found on the Galapagos Islands, or the birds of paradise Wallace studied. On a bigger scale, the giant island of Australia has evolved all sorts of amazing animals that aren't found anywhere else – kangaroos and koalas, hedgehog-like egg-laying echidnas, and duck-billed platypuses, which are so weird that when people in Britain first saw them they thought someone had stitched different animals together as a joke.

What a ridiculous looking creature!

# TRUE OR FALSE?

As well as collecting unusual animals, Charles Darwin also ate them. He had armadillos, pumas, iguanas and giant tortoises for dinner on his round-the-world voyage.

**ANSWER: True.** At university, instead of joining the debating society or something, Darwin had been a member of the Glutton Club, which met every week to eat unusual meat, including hawks and owls. His trip gave him the opportunity to try some really odd animals. One day, he and his shipmates were tucking into a tasty bird when Darwin spotted that it was a rare species that he'd only heard about, so he stopped anyone from eating what was left of it – the head and neck and a wing – and sent it back to Britain. It was later named Darwin's rhea, a type of large, flightless bird that still lives in South America. Not one of the giant tortoises captured in the Galapagos Islands made it back to Britain, because Darwin and the crew ate them. Luckily they couldn't quite manage all of the tortoises, and left some behind on the Galapagos.

# Revolutionary Evolutionary Theory

Darwin came up with most of his ideas in the 1830s, but only told a couple of friends about them. In 1858, Wallace wrote to Darwin telling him about his own theories, and asking for help getting them published. Little did he know he was actually giving Darwin a massive kick up the behind. Wallace's ideas were so similar to his own that Darwin realised he'd better not keep quiet any longer – otherwise no one would know he'd had his theory first.

So Darwin published a scientific paper outlining his own and Wallace's ideas in 1858. Here's the short and simple version of what it said:

 All kinds of animals have to compete for food, because usually there's only a limited supply.

 All kinds of animals have to overcome danger, such as very cold or hot temperatures, or things that want to eat them.

 Individual living things of the same species are a bit different from one another. If an individual animal has a feature that helps it survive, it will live longer. If it lives longer it will probably have more babies than other animals of the same kind, so that feature is more likely to be passed on to future generations. So, for example, if an individual bird that lives on shellfish has an extra-pointy beak that means it

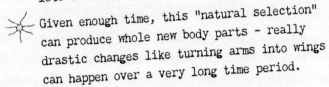

can get at shellfish more easily, it might
live longer, attract more mates, and have
lots of babies with extra-pointy beaks.

Given enough time, this "natural selection"
can produce whole new body parts - really
drastic changes like turning arms into wings
can happen over a very long time period.

Whole new species have evolved through
natural selection.

All species evolved from a common ancestor
- the first life on Earth.

Usually it takes absolutely ages for natural selection to happen. But you can see the same sort of process happening much more quickly - for example, when people breed animals to select particular features. Really fast dogs that win races have been bred to be light and lean with long legs, because people have chosen parent dogs with those features to have puppies together. In the same way, juggling dogs have been bred for their special paws. (Actually, just kidding about the juggling dogs.)

The same thing happens in the natural world, though it usually takes much longer and has nothing to do with racing or juggling, but with being better able to survive and thrive.

# THE DARWIN AND WALLACE QUIZ

**Try answering these questions about our groundbreaking, evolutionary-theory-making Victorian heroes . . .**

**1.** What did Alfred Russel Wallace find on his verandah while he was staying on the island of Borneo?

a) An infestation of venomous spiders

b) Human heads

c) Nesting birds of paradise

**2.** What's unusual about Darwin's frog, which lives in Chile and Argentina and was named after Charles Darwin?

a) It's extremely poisonous

b) It makes a sound like a barking dog

c) Its tadpoles develop inside the male frog's mouth

**3.** How many orang-utans were shot by Wallace?

a) None

b) Two

c) Sixteen

**4.** Which of these birds did Darwin study on the Galapagos Islands?

a) Red-crested twits

b) Blue-footed boobies

c) Yellow-billed bonkers

**5.** What delayed Wallace's bird-finding expedition to New Guinea?

a) Pirates

b) Cannibals

c) Man-eating sharks

**ANSWERS:**

1.     b). The local people had a habit of cutting off the heads of their enemies, then drying them out and keeping them. Wallace liked the people, and luckily they liked him too.

2.     c). The tadpoles turn into froglets inside the male frog's vocal sac. When they're ready, the male frog spits them out.

3.     c). Wallace was absolutely fantastic and brilliant in many ways, but, like other people of his time, he did have a tendency to shoot things. In those days, people thought that a good way to study animals was to examine dead ones.

4.     b). The twits and the bonkers are made up.

5.     a). Life was difficult for a specimen-hunting scientist. Wallace had to encounter all sorts of hardship on his travels, including disease, hunger, shipwreck and pirates, which delayed his search for birds of paradise for two months. Incidentally, Wallace was the first person to bring living birds of paradise to Europe – he didn't shoot *everything* – and he gave them to London Zoo. Everyone was amazed that the birds had legs, because they'd only seen dead ones which had had their legs removed.

# Evolution Wars

The idea that all life on Earth evolved from a common ancestor, and that our distant ancestors are the same as the distant ancestors of chimps and gorillas, was absolutely shocking to a lot of people. After all, their religion told them something completely different. Evolutionary ideas were often misunderstood, too, which meant the Victorians (who seem to have been pretty easily shocked) were constantly getting red in the face, or falling into faints and having to be revived with smelling salts.

Keep your hair on! Darwin said that humans and apes and monkeys have a common ancestor, which isn't the same thing at all.

# Troublesome Antlers

It's tempting to think of evolution as a long climb towards perfection, with animals getting better and better, and with human beings at the top of the heap feeling very pleased with ourselves. But evolution doesn't work like that. It's a series of random changes – if the changes prove useful (or sometimes just don't prove harmful), then the living things that inherit them will pass them on.

Sometimes animals evolve features that end up doing them more harm than good. The huge Irish elk was a type of deer which measured more than two metres tall at the shoulder. Male Irish elks' antlers got bigger and bigger – probably because female Irish elks liked the antlers so much.

Be afraid!

Male Irish elks showed them off by fighting one another, in the same way that other kinds of deer do today. The antlers ended up so enormous that they measured more than 3.6 metres across (two tall men could lie across them end to end).

Did these ginormous antlers make life better for the Irish elk? Well, not most of the time. They were heavy (40 kilograms!) and cumbersome, and it's just as well the Irish elk didn't have to walk through any doorways. The antlers must have been really annoying, apart from when the Irish elk was showing off, when they were absolutely great. The poor old Irish elk died out around eleven thousand years ago, along with its ridiculously large headgear.

## The Origin of Species

Charles Darwin wrote a famous book called *On the Origin of Species* (which became an overnight bestseller). So, what *is* the origin of species? Actually, what are species?

### ? ? ?

There are a lot of different kinds of life on Earth – living things as different as butterflies and blue whales. But imagine if there weren't. The first life on Earth could have gone on changing, evolving by natural selection, without branching off into any new species. There would be just one kind of life – let's call them dullsters. The dullsters would have to get their energy from sunlight, or something else that wouldn't run out. There wouldn't be any plants for the dullsters to eat, or any other animals, because there wouldn't be any other kinds of living thing. The dullsters would evolve as conditions on Earth changed – if it got warmer or colder, for example – and if they didn't evolve so that they adapted to the new conditions, the dullsters would die out. Things would be very, very dull indeed. But that wouldn't matter, because the dullsters probably wouldn't care, and we definitely wouldn't be around to be bored.

Luckily for us, that's not how things happened. As one group of living things changed, adapting to special conditions, it eventually became so different from the other living things that it could no longer breed with them. This is one way of saying what species are:

Species are separate groups of living things that can breed with one another and produce babies that can go on breeding, but can't breed with other groups of living thing. New species are made when two groups of the same living thing have evolved to become different enough from one another that they can't breed any more.

For example, different kinds of dog all belong to the same species, so a Labrador can breed with a poodle, but cats and dogs are different species, so a poodle can't breed with a Siamese cat. Horses and donkeys are different species, and they can breed with one another, but their babies, half horse and half donkey, can't go on to produce any more babies.

But it's more complicated than that, I'm afraid. Sometimes, very similar species can breed and produce hybrids that *can* have babies. Those creatures might be the beginning of a whole new species. And sometimes it can be difficult to say whether two groups of similar animals are the same or different species. This is the kind of thing scientists have arguments about.

There. I hope that's cleared that one up for you.

Now that we've met Mr Darwin and Mr Wallace and know about evolution and species and natural selection, let's get back to the first life on Earth . . .

# 3
# Slimy Planet

Remember the DNA – the clever self-copying molecule inside a protective case? The whole thing, including the case, is called a cell, and all living things are made of cells. The very first living things on Earth were just single cells, without all the extra bits like arms and legs and heads and stuff.

 ## Pond Life

So, were there all sorts of little wriggling cells wiggling about all over the place, furiously adapting and changing into ever more complex and wonderful creatures every week or so?

## ? ? ?

Not exactly. About 200 million years after life on Earth began, a type of bluey-green bacteria evolved that looked like the sort of stuff you might find floating on a stagnant pond. This formed most of life on Earth for around 1,400 million years. Thanks to the bacteria, the sea became full of oxygen, and oxygen released into the atmosphere made the ozone layer, which protects the Earth from harmful radiation. Think of it as a very useful but very long and slimy interlude before things really got going.

Then, just when you thought everything was going to stay that way for ever and ever and nothing interesting would EVER happen (some lessons can feel a bit like this), something DID.

Did the bacteria all get together and form a woolly mammoth or something mega-exciting like that?

## ??? 

No, of course not! Round about 2000 million years ago, more complex cells evolved called protists. There were still plenty of bacteria about, though, and there still are to this day. Just a minute – can you hear something?

# *The Bacteria's Song*

*We're all around you every day:*
*We live in your interior,*
*We're in your hair, and on your face,*
*In deep dark caves, and up in space,*
*We're everywhere – we're bacteria!*

*Some of us can do you harm –*
*We might give you diphtheria.*
*Most of us are harmless, though,*
*We help you to digest, you know.*
*You couldn't live without bacteria!*

*We're single cells, but even so*
*We won't be called inferior,*
*We've been around much longer than you,*
*There are trillions of trillions of us, too.*
*We're superior bacteria!*

Good grief, singing bacteria. But they're absolutely right. In fact, it's a staggering thought, but there are several times more bacteria inside your body than there are human cells (and there are quite a lot of those).

At this very moment, inside your gut there are more *E. coli* bacteria than the number of human beings who have ever lived. That's just one of the types of bacteria that live in your gut – there are loads. And those are just the *E. coli* bacteria living inside *you*! It's pretty staggering. All this frantic bacteria action helps us function in all sorts of ways, and without it we wouldn't survive.

And bacteria are completely rock hard . . .

- **They can live in ground that's permanently frozen.**

- **They can live in hydrothermal vents – cracks deep in the ocean where super-hot water shoots out from the depths of the Earth.**

- **There are even bacteria that live on electricity! Honestly, you couldn't make this stuff up.**

- **They've been sent up into space and still survived. Scientists are finding out whether bacteria can survive on Mars.**

So let's give bacteria a huge round of applause.

**One type of bacteria lives deep in caves, where it's mega acidic, there's no light and nothing else can live. They hang from the cave roof in slimy colonies. What are they called?**

a)   Troglobacteria

b)   Slimerella

c)   Snottites

**ANSWER:**
c) – because they're sort of a cross between stalactites and snot!

# Protists and Fungi

Anyway, back to the more complex single cells, the protists. The special thing about them is that, unlike bacteria, they have an extra bit – a "nucleus" in the middle of the cell, which surrounds the DNA (there's more about cells on page 30). Another 400 million years after they'd turned up, about 1600 million years ago, multi-celled protists evolved – the very first life that wasn't just a single cell. Whey-hey! Things were really motoring now. They're the ancestors of all living things – animals (including you), plants and fungi.

While we're on the subject, have you ever wondered why living things are divided into plants, animals and fungi? Fungi seem as though they should really just be plants, but instead they've got a whole section of their own. What's so special about mushrooms and toadstools?

Fungi don't move, which is probably why we think they should, by rights, be plants. But they're not. In fact, rather spookily, fungi are more closely related to animals than to plants. So let's hope they don't evolve into giant man-eating mushrooms or something. Unlike animals, plants make their own energy from the sun, by a process called photosynthesis. You often find fungi lurking in the dark because they don't need light as plants do – like animals, they eat food, which they break down and absorb. They're a bit like a human stomach, except turned inside out, and always live in or on their food. There are more than 1.5 million species of fungus, including things like moulds and yeasts as well as mushrooms and toadstools.

That's quite enough of that. We'll meet some of the world's first animals in Chapter Five, but first, let's take a closer look at cells and DNA . . .

# 4
# How to Build a Human Out of DNA

If you're a human being – and let's assume you are, since you're reading this – you started off as a single cell formed from an egg (from your mum) and a sperm (from your dad). Cells are like mini machines, with thousands of working parts. The working parts are enzymes, made of amino acids. Enzymes are produced, and told what to do, by DNA. So all the instructions for how to grow that cell into you, a unique human being, were already there inside the cell. Individual instructions – chunks of DNA – are called genes. According to the DNA's instructions, the cell divided, and then divided again and again into all the different types of cell in your body:

- **Some cells became bits of heart, or lung, or skin, or brain.**

- **Some became the sort of cells that do a particular job, such as delivering oxygen.**

A big animal like you, with a heart and eyes and hair and lungs and things, is incredibly complicated, with *trillions* of cells.

# The Secret Insides of Cells

## QUICK QUIZ QUESTION

**How big is the world's biggest animal cell?**

a)  As big as a pinhead

b)  As big as your little fingernail

c)  As big as a walnut

d)  As big as a melon

**ANSWER:**
d). Bird's eggs are cells, and the biggest bird's egg in the world is an ostrich egg, which is around 15 centimetres high, and weighs around two kilos.

Most cells aren't the size of an ostrich eggs, though. In fact most are smaller than the width of one strand of your hair. So here's a close-up of a typical kind of cell that your body's made of:

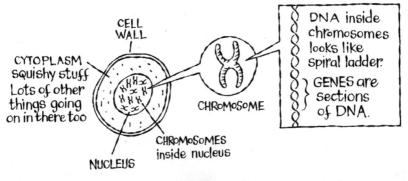

CELL WALL

CYTOPLASM squishy stuff
Lots of other things going on in there too

NUCLEUS

CHROMOSOMES inside nucleus

CHROMOSOME

DNA inside chromosomes looks like spiral ladder.

GENES are sections of DNA.

# Extract Your Own DNA!

This sounds dangerous – or at least painful – but it isn't. Honestly. However, you do need an adult to help you with this.

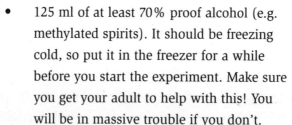

- salt

- tap water

- drinking straw

- 1 teaspoon of washing-up liquid

- 125 ml of at least 70% proof alcohol (e.g. methylated spirits). It should be freezing cold, so put it in the freezer for a while before you start the experiment. Make sure you get your adult to help with this! You will be in massive trouble if you don't.

1. Put the teaspoon of washing-up liquid and three teaspoons of water into a glass.

2. In a different glass, mix a few teaspoons of salt with water, then have a really good swill around your mouth with some of the salty water.

Spit

3. Spit out the salty water into the glass of washing-up liquid and water.

4. Slowly and carefully, stir the mixture with a clean teaspoon. Do this for a couple of minutes.

5. Very slowly and even more carefully (DON'T just slosh it in), pour the cold alcohol down the side of the glass so that it settles on top of the mixture. Leave it alone for three minutes.

6. On top of the salty washing-up liquid mixture, you should see thin white strands. Believe it or not, this is your DNA. It's amazing that it fits into the tiny nucleus of a cell.

7. You can even get the DNA out of the glass if you want to, if you've got a steady hand. Put a drinking straw into the glass and twist it slowly. The DNA strands should wrap around the straw. They break very easily so watch out. You could look at them under a microscope.

The experiment works because you spat out some of your cheek cells along with the salt water. The washing-up liquid breaks down the cheek cells, freeing the DNA. The DNA doesn't dissolve in alcohol, so it forms a solid where the salt water and alcohol meet. Anything else inside your cheek – a tiny bit of old crisp, for example – should stay dissolved in the salt water. The strands aren't just your DNA, though. The other thing we have a lot of inside our mouths is . . .

So you spat some of that out in the salty water as well. Some of the DNA belongs to the bacteria.

## Chromosomes and Sock Drawers

Imagine if all your clothes were in a big pile in the middle of your bedroom. (Obviously, that would NEVER happen in real life.) If you wanted to find your favourite T-shirt, you might have to hunt through pairs of pants and shirts and socks, and it's bound to be right in the middle, hiding underneath your embarrassing teddy-bear pyjamas (don't worry, we all have them). If you wanted to find your Superman underpants and matching tights – and that's most days for most of us – you might be searching for hours.

But if you tidy your clothes into drawers, they take up much less room and life is so much simpler. You can dress like Superman whenever you like, plus you don't have to climb over a towering pile of clothing every time you go to bed. Chromosomes are a bit like drawers – instead of the DNA being bunched up any old how and thrown into the middle of the cell, it's neatly organised into chromosomes. Now you know why you're always being nagged to tidy your room.

Chromosomes are important to you in another way: they come in pairs, and one pair determines whether you're a girl or a boy. These chromosomes look a bit like Xs and Ys: if you have two Xs – congratulations! You're a girl. And if you have an X and a Y – congratulations! You're a boy.

# THE GREAT CHROMOSOME CHALLENGE

Your task is simple: match the life form to the correct number of chromosomes (which are arranged in pairs). It sounds easy – but is it?

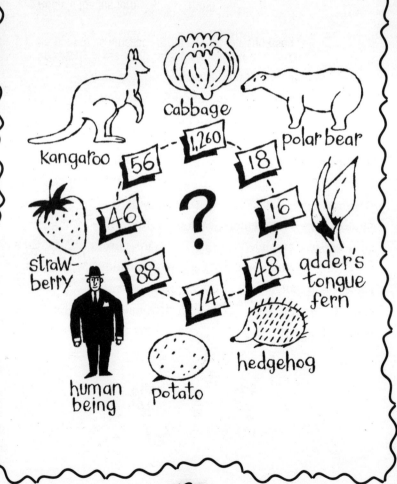

kangaroo
cabbage
polar bear

56
1,260
18

strawberry
46
?
16
adder's tongue fern

88
74
48

human being
potato
hedgehog

**ANSWERS:**

Prepare to be amazed — or at least mildly surprised . . .

| Adder's tongue fern | 1,260 |
| Hedgehog | 88 |
| Polar bear | 74 |
| Strawberry | 56 |
| Potato | 48 |
| Human being | 46 |
| Cabbage | 18 |
| Kangaroo | 16 |

Incidentally, the adder's tongue fern has the highest number of chromosomes of any living thing, by quite a long way. But what's so special about it? Why do strawberries have the same number of chromosomes as elephants? And why do hedgehogs, strawberries and elephants have more chromosomes than we do? Even potatoes have more chromosomes than us, for goodness' sake! What are they hiding? Behind that potato-ey exterior, are they secretly evil geniuses plotting to take over the world with their friends the ferns and the polar bears?

Probably not. The number of chromosomes a living thing has is due to random mistakes. Sometimes two chromosomes join together to make one, and sometimes chromosomes can be copied. Either way, it doesn't mean that any information is lost, or any new information is added, just that creatures end up with more or fewer chromosomes. If there's a small number of one type of species (say there was just one small tribe of human beings in the whole world, for example), the changed number of chromosomes might spread to the whole population, again by chance. But if a single human being today has a different number of chromosomes, then the number of chromosomes of most people stays the same, because there are so many of us.

# Mutants!

Our old friends Darwin and Wallace knew that inheritance happened but didn't know how. Today we do. The first person to work it out was Gregor Mendel, an Austrian monk who lived in the 1800s. He spent a lot of time – and I mean a lot – breeding pea plants and studying the results. Thank goodness he didn't find it as dull as it sounds, because without him we wouldn't know about genes. So let's give Mendel a great big cheer. This is what he found out . . .

- Pea plants have different features — just like you do. The features of pea plants include things like stem length, flower colour and pod shape — not like you at all (at least, I hope not).

- These different features are passed on in chunks of coded information inside DNA. We now call these information chunks "genes" (Mendel didn't call them that, though), which are sections of DNA.

- For each feature (e.g. flower colour), a plant will have two genes. The two genes might be the same (two purple genes, or two pink genes), or different (one pink gene and one purple gene).

- Each parent plant passes on one gene for the same feature, so the baby pea plant will also have two genes for each feature.

- Let's say that our baby pea plant gets the gene for having pink flowers from parent plant number 1, and the gene for having purple flowers from parent plant number 2.

- So will the baby pea plant have pink or purple flowers? Well, of each pair of genes, one is stronger (dominant) and the other is weaker (recessive). Both dominant and recessive genes can be passed on, but if the baby gets one of each then the dominant gene will be the one which shows.

- Let's say that the purple gene is dominant and the pink gene is recessive. The baby will have purple flowers.

- BUT this doesn't mean that the baby's offspring will all have purple flowers. It has two different genes for flower colour, and it might pass on its pink gene to its own baby. If the other parent pea plant also passes on a pink gene, then the new baby pea plant will have pink flowers. So two purple-flowered parent plants can have a pink-flowered baby.

All those hours in the greenhouse had been worth it: Mendel had solved the problem of how all living things inherit characteristics. In the middle of the twentieth century, scientists including Francis Crick and James Watson discovered how genes are stored in DNA, and how DNA copies itself. Thanks to them, we now know what DNA looks like – a structure called a double helix, like a ladder that's been twisted into a spiral.

# THE ZORGLE GENETIC PUZZLE

Have you ever heard of a zorgle? They're unusual creatures – in fact they only exist inside the fevered brain of the illustrator of this book. But they inherit characteristics from their parents in the same way that pea plants and people and other living things do. We've created them especially so that you can have a go at solving this genetic puzzle . . .

## THINGS YOU SHOULD KNOW ABOUT A ZORGLE'S GENES:

- Hairy tentacles are dominant; bald tentacles are recessive

- Straight tails are dominant; curly tails are recessive

- Five eyes are dominant; three eyes are recessive

- Stinky drool is, unfortunately, dominant; non-stinky drool is recessive

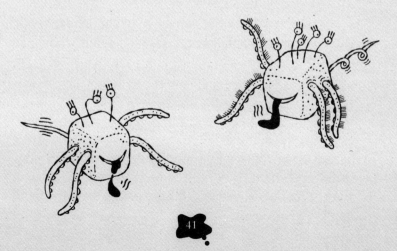

## MUM ZORGLE →

Mum passes on genes for:
• bald tentacles (Mum Zorgle has
one gene for bald tentacles, and
one gene for hairy tentacles, and
can pass either on to her baby. Her own tentacles are
hairy because hairy tentacles are dominant.)
• curly tail    • five eyes    • non-stinky drool

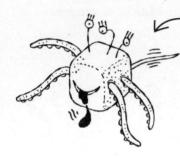

## ← DAD ZORGLE

Dad passes on genes for:
• bald tentacles    • straight tail
• three eyes    • non-stinky drool

# WHAT WILL THEIR BABY LOOK LIKE?

Answer: Baby Zorgle has . . .

- Bald tentacles, because she inherits bald tentacles from her mum, and bald ones from her dad.

- A straight tail, because she inherits one of each, but straight tails are dominant.

- Five eyes – again, she inherits both genes but the one for five eyes is dominant.

- Happily, non-stinky drool. Although her parents both have stinky drool, Baby Zorgle has non-stinky drool because they both very thoughtfully passed on a non-stinky drool gene. If either one of them had passed on a stinky drool gene, she would have ended up with stinky drool.

Just a minute, though. What's all this got to do with mutants?

A mutation is a permanent change in a living thing's genes, and it can happen when DNA is copied as cells divide. Mutations are rare, but when they happen they can change a living thing's characteristics. Sometimes it's pretty drastic – for example, the common fruit fly occasionally has a mutation that makes legs grow out of its head instead of antennae. That must be annoying, though it does make headstands a lot easier.

**Why are scientists who study genetics so keen on fruit flies?**

a) Because fruit flies are so adorably cute.

b) Because fruit flies don't live very long. That means there are lots of generations to study in a very short space of time, so scientists can watch evolution in action.

b). Have you ever seen a fruit fly? They are not adorably cute.

**ANSWER:**

Often mutations are hardly noticeable, or don't make any difference to the creature's survival. For example, different coloured eyes first appeared due to mutations. What colour are your eyes? Really? That sounds lovely! Obviously, that adds to your unique beauty, but does it help you to see any better? No, of course it doesn't.

But sometimes mutations can turn out to be useful – a tiger's stripes are due to a mutant gene. Tigers with stripes are better camouflaged in long grass and dappled sunshine, so more stripey tigers survived longer and had more cubs, over lots of generations, and now all tigers have stripes. This is the "natural selection" Darwin and Wallace talked about.

Useful mutations like a tiger's stripes, plus a few random mutations that turn up here and there, are how evolution happens.

## SO . . . YOU'RE A MUTANT!

**Every change since the very first life form has been a mutation. All of us are mutants because mutated genes have made humans (and everything else) evolve.**

# 5

# Things Get Complicated

It took thousands of millions of years for life on Earth to evolve and become more than just single cells. But after the first life evolved that had more than just one cell, things started whooshing along much more quickly.

## QUICK QUIZ QUESTION

**Scientists sometimes describe the Earth between about 750 and 580 million years ago as . . .**

a) Snowball Earth, because it was icy.

b) Doughnut Earth, because it had a hole in the middle.

c) Teardrop Earth, because it was watery, salty and warm.

d) Fireball Earth, because it was extremely hot.

**ANSWER:**
b). The Earth looked just like a doughnut, and was even coated in sugar. NOT REALLY. The answer's a) – it was almost completely covered in ice, some of it hundreds of metres thick, for periods of millions of years during this time. There were probably earlier periods of extreme icy chilliness too. Luckily, enough living things could survive in the cold and went on to evolve into the first animals . . .

# Animals at Last

Strange, soft-bodied animals evolved during Snowball Earth. Their fossils look a bit like this:

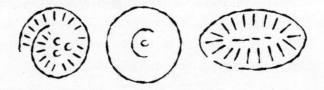

Scientists tend to scratch their heads over them, because they're not sure what they might have looked like before they were fossilised, or whether some of them died out completely. Some scientists think there were animals before Snowball Earth, and the icy conditions did most of them no favours at all. But anyway, even though we don't know very much about them, let's give the Snowball Earth animals a big pat on their soft, squishy backs because without them we wouldn't be here.

# The Cambrian Explosion

Planet Earth got warmer and more alarming – volcanoes were erupting all over the place as an enormous supercontinent formed and then bits began to break off it. But volcanoes weren't the only things exploding – so was life. Around 540 million years ago, in the Cambrian period, the ancestors of most of the major groups of animals that we know today suddenly evolved.

Well, "suddenly" is a bit of an exaggeration – most of them evolved at the beginning of the Cambrian, within about 13 million years. But when you compare it to the 1,400 million years that life on Earth consisted mainly of green slime, it's pretty sudden. There were no land animals or plants, but life in the sea was going bananas . . .

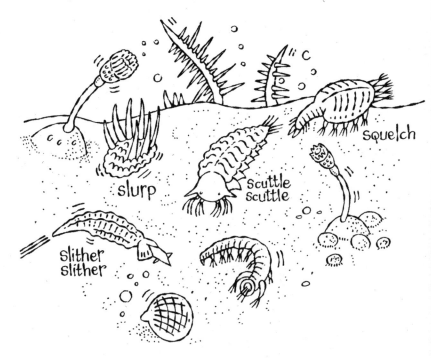

squelch

slurp

scuttle
scuttle

slither
slither

Some of it was so weird scientists spent ages working out which way up it went!

There were things with legs, spines, mouths and suckers, things that scuttled, things that burrowed themselves in the sand, things that hunted, and things that swam away as fast as they could but quite often got eaten anyway. Some had hard shells and, even more thrilling, some had eyes. Goodness, this is a bit more like it – proper animals at last. Let's meet some of the most common animals in the Cambrian . . .

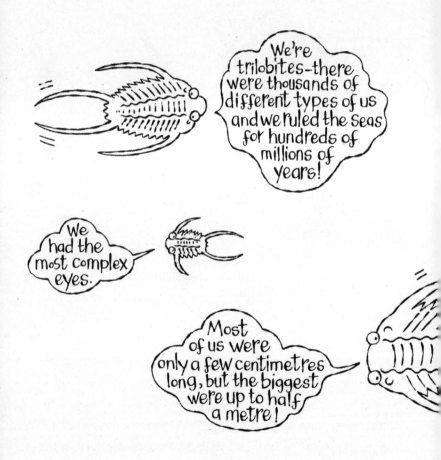

Perhaps even more exciting (no offence, trilobites), the first animals with backbones evolved during the Cambrian. Humans are animals with backbones, too, but these weren't much like us: they were jawless fish, a bit like today's hagfish, which look like eels and are pretty revolting. Hagfish are the world's slimiest animal, and they spend their time feeding inside the decaying bodies of dead sea creatures. And they wonder why they never get invited to parties.

# QUICK QUIZ QUESTION

**The Cambrian period was followed by . . .**

a)   the Big Bloom, when the first plants appeared.

b)   the Dead Interval, when lots of things died out.

c)   the Age of the Dinosaurs, when dinosaurs ruled the Earth.

d)   the Doughnut Interlude, when creatures with holes in the middle appeared for a short time.

**ANSWER:**

b). The Earth got very hot, and there were even more volcanic eruptions. Lots of things died out, so scientists call it the Dead Interval. Luckily for us, not everything died out, and soon there was another explosion of life to make up for it . . .

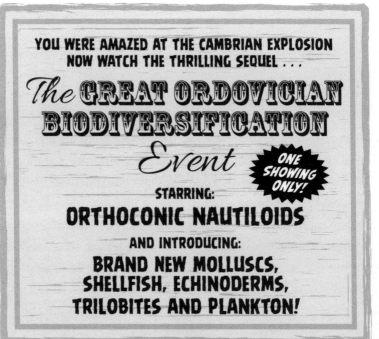

YOU WERE AMAZED AT THE CAMBRIAN EXPLOSION
NOW WATCH THE THRILLING SEQUEL . . .

*The* GREAT ORDOVICIAN BIODIVERSIFICATION *Event*

ONE SHOWING ONLY!

STARRING:
**ORTHOCONIC NAUTILOIDS**

AND INTRODUCING:
**BRAND NEW MOLLUSCS, SHELLFISH, ECHINODERMS, TRILOBITES AND PLANKTON!**

The Great Ordovician Biodiversification Event sounds very clever, so you should probably practise saying it in case you ever want to really impress someone (you could just drop it into the conversation casually). But first make sure you know what it means:

- Ordovician is the time period – it lasted about 45 million years, from roughly 488 to 443 million years ago.

- 'Biodiversification' means an increase in different kinds of life.

- And it was a Great Event because absolutely loads of different kinds of life appeared within a mere 25 million years (starting at the beginning of the Ordovician).

Most of the different life forms that evolved during the Great Ordovician Biodiversification Event were new types of creatures that were already there – for example, lots of new kinds of plankton (really tiny floating plants and animals), molluscs (snail-type things), echinoderms (creatures like today's starfish, sea urchins and sand dollars), and corals.

Our old friends the trilobites were still around, and new ones appeared, but gradually a new type of shellfish took over from them. New predators called orthoconic nautiloids, which could measure 6 metres or even longer, evolved to become top of the food chain and feast on the tasty new creatures. The

Grr!

climate in the Ordovician was very warm, which meant sea levels were high and there were lots of shallow seas covering the land – just the right conditions for plenty of plankton, and the creatures that liked eating it, and the creatures that liked eating the plankton eaters . . . So that's probably one of the reasons the Great Ordovician Biodiversification Event happened.

# Land Ahoy!

All these spines and shells and backbones and things are incredibly impressive, especially when you compare them to bacteria, but they all had one thing in common: they were sea creatures. When were land animals going to turn up?

The first creatures that crawled onto the land were arthropods (the group of animals that includes spiders, crabs and insects), and looked a bit like modern millipedes. They wriggled up out of the sea around 15 million years after the end of the Ordovician period, about 428 million years ago. They joined the first land plants, which were a type of fern and gradually evolved into all sorts of new plants. At the same time, new predators appeared to join the scary orthoconic nautiloids: giant sea scorpions, up to 2.5 metres long, were lying in wait on the seabed to snap up some of the delicious new fish that had evolved.

But human beings didn't evolve from the first land animals, the ancient millipede-like creatures. The first land animals that were our ancestors were called tetrapods, and they looked like this:

# ?? QUICK QUIZ QUESTION ??

**Which of these modern creatures are classed as tetrapods?**

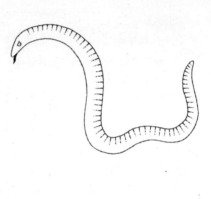

a) Pigeons

b) Human beings

c) Whales

d) Frogs

e) Snakes

**ANSWER:**

All of them, even though they all don't have four legs at all. In fact, two of them don't have any legs at all. They're all descended from early tetrapods, the ancestors of amphibians, reptiles, dinosaurs (including birds) and mammals, and are classed as tetrapods. All today's land animals with backbones are related to the ancient tetrapods. Some sea creatures are, too, such as turtles and whales. They were land animals for a while before they decided that life in the sea was a much better idea, and gradually returned to living in the ocean like their ancestors.

# ANOTHER QUICK QUIZ QUESTION

Like other tetrapods, humans have red blood cells that carry oxygen around our bodies. What shape are the red blood cells?

a)   Worm-shaped

b)   Star-shaped

c)   Square

d)   Doughnut-shaped

**ANSWER:**

d). They look like round, squishy doughnuts with a dent in the middle. There's no jam in them, though. You knew that "doughnut" had to be the right answer at some point, didn't you?

Our earliest ancestors who lived on land were scampering about roughly 360 million years ago. Obviously, there was still quite a long way to go between these first tetrapods and human beings, but we are a bit closer to making a human out of soup. Just another few hundreds of millions of years of evolution still to go.

First, amphibians branched off from the rest of the tetrapods to turn into frogs, toads, salamanders and things. Then, the remaining four-legged animals split into two separate kinds of reptiles. One lot became your ancestors, the other lot were dinosaurs, and we'll be saying hello to them later on.

# 6

# Rocks and Fossils

Leap into your time machine again and set the dial to zero, because we're going back to planet Earth when it first formed.

## Cheese-on-Toast Earth and Soup Continents

While we're waiting for the time machine to make bleeping noises and wibble about a bit in preparation for its journey, go and make yourself some cheese on toast. You'll know when it's just about ready because the surface of the cheese starts to bubble away nicely. That's what the surface of planet Earth was like in the beginning – molten, bubbling and sizzling. Except it was surrounded by evil-smelling gases, and not nearly as tasty.

Unlike the cheese on toast, it took around 500 million years for the Earth to cool down a bit. (You can eat the cheese on toast now.) By this time the planet had an intensely hot, molten core of nickel-iron, another very hot layer on top of that, and finally the Earth's crust, covered in water and land – the primordial soup. In the thousands of millions of years since then, the land has shifted about dramatically – though very slowly.

This is because of the movement of the crust, which is made up of big chunks, known as tectonic plates, that push and grind against one another, pushing up mountain ranges and causing huge volcanic eruptions, earthquakes and tsunamis.

So, if you stop your time machine at year zero, you'll see the bubbling cheese-on-toast Earth, then keep skipping hundreds of millions of years forwards and you'll see the land arranged in different patterns, sometimes coming together in one place to form one giant continent, and then splitting apart again. If you're still hungry, or if your time machine's temporarily out of action, make some soup (it can be any flavour except primordial), scatter a few pieces of bread on the top (these are the continents) and swirl them about a bit to see a similar effect.

# Drifting Continents

The most recent giant continent that we know about formed roughly 300 million years ago. Scientists call it Pangaea, and it included all the land we know today – Africa, India, Europe, the Americas, Australia and Antarctica – in one massive lump, in the southern half of the world. Roughly 200 million years ago, during the time of the dinosaurs, it very slowly started to break apart and spread out. The dinosaurs didn't find themselves sailing about on the sea, and bashing into other chunks of land with other marooned dinosaurs on them, or anything like that – they didn't notice the land moving about at all, because it was happening so slowly. We don't notice it either: today the tectonic plates are still moving, so that in millions of years' time the continents will be squashed together in a huge supercontinent once again.

A German scientist called Alfred Wegener came up with the idea of continents moving about – or "continental drift" – in 1912, when he noticed how the east coast of South America fits quite neatly into the west coast of Africa, like jigsaw pieces. He also noticed shared rocks and fossils – for example, fossils from a land animal called *Cynognathus* have been found in western Africa and the middle bit of South America. Wegener realised that it lived when the two continents were joined together and the Atlantic Ocean didn't exist, so it didn't have to swim for thousands of kilometres.

And speaking of fossils . . .

# Fossils!

The only reason we know about trilobites and giant sea scorpions and other ancient extinct creatures is because of fossils. But what are they exactly?

## ? ? ?

They're not the bones of dead creatures that have been preserved, because even bone rots away eventually. Fossils are the remains of ancient plants and animals (and more rarely bacteria and fungi), and they need particular conditions to form. Although there are loads of them in museums around the world, they're only a tiny fraction of the life that existed, and there are probably tons of creatures that we'll never know about because they were never fossilised.

Let's pop back to 20 million years ago and find out what could happen to this fish:

# Scenario number 1

Our fish had a long and happy life, when one day it got crunched by a megalodon – a 16-metre-long shark that's now extinct – as a light appetiser before its main course of a fairly large whale. Would that make a fossil?

No, it wouldn't. Incidentally, we only know about megalodons because of their teeth – like other sharks, their bodies are made from cartilage, which is soft and doesn't become fossilised because it rots away too quickly, so no complete megalodon fossils exist, just their ginormous gnashers.

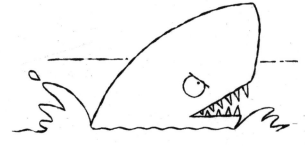

# Scenario number 2

Our fish has managed to avoid getting munched by predators, and finally dies of old age. It drifts down to the seabed and, as it does so, various creatures take a bite out of it so that its bones are scattered far and wide, and crunched up inside other sea creatures. Would that make a fossil?

No, of course it wouldn't.

# Scenario number 3

Our fish has managed to avoid predators, and finally dies of old age in an especially quiet area of the sea. It floats to the bottom, where a nice layer of sand gets gently deposited on top of it, protecting it from harm before the fish's skeleton can get swept away by the swish of a large animal's tail, or trodden on or swept away by a wave. Many thousands of years later, the water pressure has made the sand into sandstone. The bony skeleton has dissolved away, leaving gaps that become filled by minerals. Finally, millions of years of erupting volcanoes push the sandstone up on to dry land, and the fish fossil is discovered by a passing human being.

So, really, becoming fossilised isn't verylikely. That's why people get so excited about fossils – not only do they show us living things that lived long ago and don't exist today, but they're the result of millions of years of luck.

There are particular places on Earth that are full of fossils, like the south coast of England, which is known as the Jurassic Coast because of all the dinosaur-age fossils that are found there. Later on, we'll have a dig about in the Messel Pit in Germany, where there are lots of fossils from a different time period. In these places, conditions were once just right for making fossils.

There are other ways of ancient creatures becoming preserved – in very icy, or very dry conditions, for example. And you never know what gruesome discoveries you might find in a peat bog – conditions inside them can preserve living things for thousands of years, and hundreds of "bog bodies" have been found, preserved men, women and children. We'll meet some other, much more ancient human beings later on.

The most common fossils include trilobites and sea creatures with spiral shells called ammonites. Others are very rare – some prehistoric creatures are only known about from one small bit of fossilised bone. In fact it's quite unusual to find a fossil that's got all its bits and pieces. If one's found that's almost all there – especially if it's a big one or a rare one – everyone practically faints on the spot with excitement. These kinds of fossils can be sold for vast sums of money – the most expensive one ever was a *Tyrannosaurus rex* fossil, nicknamed Sue after the scientist who discovered it. It's one of the biggest and best-preserved *T. rex* fossils ever found, and it was bought by the Field Museum of Natural History in Chicago, USA, for $8.36 million in 1997.

# Make Your Own Fossil

**You need:**
- Modelling clay (e.g. plasticine)
- PVA glue
- A small, flat-ish shell, or a twig, or anything else that will make a fairly shallow impression in the clay. This is standing in for a dead *T. rex*, so you'll also need . . .
- A fair bit of imagination

**1** Make an impression in the clay with your object – don't make it too deep, or your fossil will take a long time to harden.

**2** Gently remove the object without squishing the clay, so that it leaves an almost perfect imprint of the object. Imagine that a *T. rex* dropped dead after a vicious fight with a particularly tough *Triceratops*, and over time its body has rotted away, leaving the impression. As I said, you'll need a bit of imagination.

3 Carefully fill up the clay impression with PVA glue. You have to imagine that these are minerals slowly seeping into the rock to form a fossil.

4 Leave the glue overnight to harden. Depending on how deep it is, it might take more or less time than that to harden properly.

5 Once the glue's dry, carefully remove it from the clay – you might need to cut off some of the excess glue. Imagine you're a palaeontologist carefully chipping away rock to expose the fossil. You should see all of the features of your object in your glue fossil.

This is only really half a fossil – obviously a real *T. rex* wouldn't be flat on top like the glue. But you get the idea.

There are other ways that prehistoric creatures can tell us about their existence – footprints, burrows or trails left by ancient animals are known as trace fossils. Coprolites are bits of fossilised ancient poo – and to some scientists, these are surprisingly fascinating. And sometimes very small creatures got stuck in tree resin, which hardened to become amber, preserving the animal's body for millions of years.

# Living Fossils

Most fossils are only bones and teeth (though there are a few where some of the skin, fur or stomach contents has been preserved), and we have to guess what the creatures looked like when they were alive. But we have a pretty good idea of what some animal fossils looked like when they were alive, because creatures just like them are still alive today: some things are incredibly tough and have survived almost unchanged for millions of years. An example is the coelacanth, an ugly-looking fish.

Oi! Who you calling ugly?

Everyone thought coelacanths had died out at the same time as the dinosaurs, 65 million years ago, until someone caught a live one in a fishing net the 1930s. They are huge – up to two metres long – and still live deep in the oceans off the coasts of East Africa and Indonesia.

Coelacanths may be ugly, but they're interesting in lots of ways, and one of them is because of their fins. Yes, really. The coelacanth's fins are long and move one after the other, like a pair of legs – they're part-way between a normal fish's fins and the stumpy legs that allowed the first backboned animals to slither up out of the sea and onto dry land. The coelacanths must have decided they liked being the way they were, though, because they're still almost exactly the same as coelacanth fossils millions of years old.

The sad thing is that coelacanths are now an endangered species – after all those millions of years of sticking around, they might finally be about to die out, and we've hardly even got to know one another yet.

There are living fossil plants too. One is the ginkgo tree, which has been around for at least 200 million years – since the time of the dinosaurs – and has stayed almost identical ever since. Individual trees can live for absolutely ages – the oldest ginkgo tree recorded is an astonishing 3,500 years old. Ginkgos are the only surviving plants of their type, and, not surprisingly, they're incredibly tough.

# TRUE OR FALSE?

Ginkgo trees are tough enough to survive a nuclear blast.

Answer: Incredible but true. Some ginkgo trees survived close to where a nuclear bomb was dropped at Hiroshima in Japan. Nothing else survived, but the ginkgo trees are still there today. They are truly the hard nuts of the plant world, and deserve some kind of medal at the very least.

# Dragons!

When people found the first fossils, no one had any idea what they were, and there were all sorts of strange ideas about them . . .

🌸 Lots of people didn't believe that any animals could have died out, because they thought that God created the world just as it is and it would always stay the same. So the fossil remains of things like giant sea monsters were a puzzle. People thought fossils were the remains of creatures that must still exist somewhere on Earth – hiding in the deepest oceans, perhaps (which actually isn't such a crazy idea – we're still discovering new species deep in the ocean even now).

🌸 People suggested that belemnite fossils – the remains of squid-like creatures with internal shells – were thunderbolts thrown by the gods.

Different fossils were thought to be different bits of the Devil – or maybe, since there are a lot of them, his little demon helpers. Ammonites, the spiral-shell fossils, were Devil's horns, fossilised sharks' teeth were Devil's teeth, and fossil brachiopods, a bit like modern mussel shells, were Devil's claws.

In the stones of the pyramids at Giza are the fossils of single-celled animals with shells that lived on the seabed. When the Romans visited the pyramids 2000 years ago – which was 2500 years after they were built – they thought the fossils were the remains of the food of the workers who'd built the pyramids.

Fossils were often seen as proof that dragons really existed. One in particular looks quite a lot like legendary dragons – it's called *Dracorex hogwartsia*. (Incidentally, it was named *hogwartsia* in honour of the Harry Potter books.)

Fossil bones of dwarf elephants were found in caves around the Mediterranean. The skulls have a big hole in them (for the elephant's trunk), and it's thought that the Ancient Greeks came up with stories of one-eyed monsters, called Cyclopes, because of them. In the same way, stories about the mythical griffin, half lion and half eagle, might have been because of the discovery of dinosaur skulls and other bones.

Fossils of sea creatures found high up in mountain ranges were especially puzzling. Actually they're proof of how much the Earth has changed, as continents move and collide and what used to be the seabed ends up halfway up a mountain.

# Hard Evidence

Fossils are evidence of how animals have evolved over time. Not surprisingly, Charles Darwin collected fossils, and one of the absolute favourites of his collection must have been the amazing *Megatherium*. Darwin found the fossilised head of this huge mammal while he was in South America on his round-the-world trip in the 1830s. It belonged to an extinct giant ground sloth that weighed around the same as a humpback whale, and it would have been able to reach inside a first-floor window, if buildings had existed at the time.

Darwin realised that the sloths that were alive and well in South America while he was there were related to the extinct ones, though they'd become an awful lot smaller. It helped convince him of how animals change over time.

# 7

# Extinction, Dinosaurs, Mammals, and Extinction Again

You know how it is: there's a massive explosion of new life forms and then, just when everything's evolving nicely . . . WHUMP! Everything's wiped out in an instant. Typical!

## The Great Dying

There have been a few mass extinctions in the history of the Earth. One of them happened at the end of the Ordovician, around 440 million years ago, but the one that happened around 250 million years ago was the most devastating of all (even though there's a later one that's much more famous, which you can find out about on page 78). It's known as the End-Permian Mass Extinction, or, more dramatically, the Great Dying, and probably happened over a few million years.

Temperatures on Earth were very hot, and got even hotter after an enormous volcanic eruption, which went on for hundreds of thousands of years and changed the gases in the atmosphere. The sea warmed up, releasing more gases that made the temperature hotter still. Meanwhile, there was less oxygen in the sea, killing off creatures that relied on it and also the creatures that preyed on them. All in all, things were hot, gassy, and absolutely lethal to a lot of life on Earth.

## QUICK QUIZ QUESTION

**What percentage of Earth's species was wiped out in the Great Dying?**

a)   More than 30 per cent

b)   More than 50 per cent

c)   More than 70 per cent

d)   More than 90 per cent

**ANSWER:**

d). About 95 per cent of species that existed at the time were completely wiped out in the mass extinction that happened around 250 million years ago.

Some of our old friends were gone for good: the trilobites had been around for nearly 300 million years, and had survived two earlier mass extinctions, but they finally bit the dust in the Great Dying, and so did the giant sea scorpions we met on page 52. Land animals were affected too, and even insects got nobbled. Insects are the hard nuts of the animal kingdom, and it's the only time in Earth's history that huge numbers of different kinds of insect all died out at the same time.

So today's living things are descended from the tiny minority that somehow managed to survive. When you think about it, it's exceptionally lucky for us that our own ancestors weren't wiped out as well, otherwise we wouldn't be here. And if the Great Dying hadn't happened, maybe something would have evolved that ate all our ancestors, in which case we wouldn't be here either. Although it was a fatal few million years for most of life on Earth, it was a piece of luck for us humans.

# Splitting Tetrapods

Remember our ancestors, the early tetrapods? They carried on evolving and split into separate groups. There were amphibians, and two different types of reptile. One kind of reptile became dinosaurs, and another became mammal-like reptiles, which are our ancestors. But can you tell which is which?

It may not look much like you or anyone you know (at least I hope not), but the one on the left is your distant ancestor. It's called *Dimetrodon*, and it lived a bit earlier than the first dinosaurs. This kind of reptile evolved into more and more mammal-like creatures, until they started to evolve things like whiskers and fur, and lost the huge sail-like thing on its back (thank goodness – it would only get in the way).

## Mammals Turn Up

What do you have in common with a camel, a whale and a hedgehog?

We're all animals!

We're all animals with backbones!

We all have cells! And DNA and genes!

OK, so there are actually quite a few things. Anything else?

We're all mammals!

Yes! And even though us mammals can be very different from one another, we're all descended from the same creatures that evolved more than 200 million years ago. Some of the first mammals to evolve looked like small rats.

Scientists argue over which animals were the first true mammals, and exactly when they first appeared . . . and all sorts of other things. Which isn't surprising, since it all happened hundreds of millions of years ago, and it can be tricky piecing together bits of fossilised bone and deciding which bit goes where and which animals had fur and which laid eggs, and that kind of thing.

Hang on. Did you just hear a sort of stomping sound? Hmmm . . . well, let's not worry about it, it was probably nothing.

These are the features that make us mammals:

### We have backbones.

### We feed milk to our babies.

### We have warm blood.

### We are hairy (this varies quite a bit).

Along with lions and rhinos and dogs, us human beings can trace our ancestry back to a small, ratty, insect-eating creature with a long tail.

**THUMP!**

There was that noise again! While the first mammals were snuffling and scampering about, another type of creature ruled the world . . . In fact, quick! Hide behind that rock! Something enormous is heading this way!

## Dinosaur World

Like us mammals, the dinosaurs also started off as those early tetrapods we met on page 53. Millions of years of evolution made them turn out a bit differently from the mammals, though. We might tend to think of them as massive great monsters like *T. rex* or *Stegosaurus*, but there was a wide variety, because dinosaurs were around for a very, very long time. By the way, I think it's safe to come out from behind the rock now.

## TRUE OR FALSE?

**Which of these statements about dinosaurs are true?**

1. Crocodiles are descended from dinosaurs.
2. Pterosaurs were flying dinosaurs.
3. Plesiosaurs – which look like the legendary animal in Loch Ness – were sea dinosaurs.
4. Birds are descended from pterosaurs.

The first dinosaurs appeared around 230 million years ago, during the Mesozoic Era, and carried on evolving, and getting bigger or smaller, or sprouting feathers or horns or special head crests and things, for a staggering 160 million years. Some were absolutely huge – the biggest dinosaur fossil discovered so far was unearthed in Argentina in 2014. It's reckoned to have been 26 metres long and weighed nearly 60 tonnes (the equivalent of twelve African elephants) . . . and it wasn't even fully grown! Scientists have called it *Dreadnoughtus*, which means "fear nothing". It probably didn't fear anything as it stomped around South America eating vast quantities of plant life.

At the other end of the dinosaur scale, *Epidexipteryx* is one of the smallest dinosaurs – it was only about the size of a pigeon. And, like pigeons, it had feathers.

As well as the mammals, other creatures evolved to share the Earth with the dinosaurs – flying reptiles called pterosaurs swooped about the skies looking really scary. In the sea, all sorts of new fish were frantically trying to avoid massive predators like mosasaurs, ichthyosaurs and plesiosaurs. Joining the fish on the seafood menu were creatures that would later evolve into crabs, lobsters and prawns, and there were also sea snails and starfish-like animals.

In the middle of the age of the dinosaurs there was another mass extinction, but that one wasn't quite so devastating, at least not to the dinosaurs (eel-like creatures called conodonts, sea-snail-type things and big amphibians all came out of it very badly, though). Then suddenly, after all those millions of years of dinosaurs, it happened again – and this one did affect the dinosaurs. Sixty-five million years ago, the dinosaurs disappeared, along with their pterosaur friends and a number of frightening sea creatures – in fact, almost all big animals with backbones.

There are different theories about what happened: one is that there was a huge . . .

**THWACK!**

. . . as an absolutely enormous asteroid or comet came whumping into the Earth. The impact caused huge tsunamis, and massive clouds of dust that blocked out the sun, and lots of animals couldn't cope with the changes (never mind the ones who couldn't cope with being hit by an enormous asteroid). There's a huge crater in Mexico that dates from around 65 million years ago, which makes it look as though this theory is right.

The extinction might not have been caused by the asteroid hit on its own, though. It's also true that lots of groups of dinosaurs and other big animals hadn't been doing so well anyway. Maybe the asteroid was just the final straw. And it might be that the extinctions were also helped along by volcanic eruptions and climate change too.

But no one really knows exactly what caused the extinction. And there are other mysteries – for example, how come frogs and other amphibians managed to survive when they're so picky about the conditions they live in, while stonking great tough nuts like *Tyrannosaurus rex* bit the dust?

# EXTINCTION QUIZ

It's a mind-boggling thought, but 99 per cent of all the animals that have ever lived are now extinct. Some of them died out in mass extinctions, like the Great Dying at the end of the Permian, or the mass extinction that wiped out the dinosaurs. But most of them died out because conditions on Earth changed and they couldn't adapt quickly enough – and some of this is down to us human beings and how we've changed things to suit us. Try this extinction quiz and find out how much you know about extinct animals . . .

1. **_Sarcosuchus_ is an extinct giant . . . ?**
a) Flightless bird
b) Sea snake-like animal
c) Crocodile-like animal

2. **The flightless dodo has been extinct since the 1600s, within a hundred years of its discovery on the island of Mauritius by Europeans. Which of these birds is it closely related to?**

a) Pigeons
b) Eagles
c) Ostriches

3. **The dingo proved to be a more successful predator and drove which of these now extinct animals out of Australia?**
a) The Tasmanian Devil
b) The Nullarbor wolf
c) The thylacine

4. **What kind of animal was the extinct _Titanoboa_?**
a) A giant kangaroo
b) A giant snake
c) A giant beetle

5. **Woolly mammoths were a bit like modern elephants, but they were very hairy and . . .**
a) They had small ears
b) They didn't have tusks
c) They were only half the size

**6.** **Which of these were a common sight in Madagascar until the 1600s?**

a) Elephant mice

b) Elephant lemurs

c) Elephant birds

**7.** **The extinct broad-faced potoroo was most similar to which of these?**

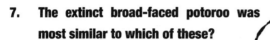

a) A miniature kangaroo

b) A giant rabbit

c) A miniature elephant

**8.** **Passenger pigeons were North America's most common bird when the first European settlers arrived. How many were there in 1914?**

a) One

b) Ten

c) A hundred

**9.** **Which of these is a real animal that's facing extinction today?**

a) Sad-faced woolly sloth

b) Gloomy tube-nosed bat

c) Murky owl-eyed lizard

**10.** **Which of these animals are in danger of becoming extinct in the wild?**

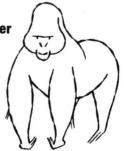

a) Black rhino

b) Mountain gorilla

c) Leatherback turtle

# ANSWERS:

**1. c).** *Sarcosuchus* was an absolutely massive crocodile-like animal. Today's saltwater crocodiles are enormous and would happily eat you for breakfast, but *Sarcosuchus* was twice their size, at nearly twelve metres long. *Sarcosuchus* lived around 110 million years ago.

**2. a).** The dodo was easy to catch because it couldn't fly, but apparently it didn't taste that nice, and was likely driven to extinction because of the animals that the Europeans brought with them to Mauritius, not because they ate them all. The dodo's closest relatives, pigeons, have been identified with the help of DNA research.

**3. c).** The thylacine was a meat-eating, stripy, wolf-like animal with a pouch like a kangaroo's – just one of Australia's weird and wonderful creatures. It became extinct in Australia about three thousand years ago, but was alive and well in Tasmania until the twentieth century, when it finally died out completely. The Tasmanian Devil is a different type of animal that still lives in Tasmania (it's now endangered), and there's no such thing as the Nullarbor wolf.

**4. b).** The *Titanoboa* lived about 60 million years ago and was, as far as we know, the biggest snake that's ever lived. It measured about 14 metres long and was massively thick. Like modern anacondas and pythons, it wasn't venomous but squeezed its prey to death.

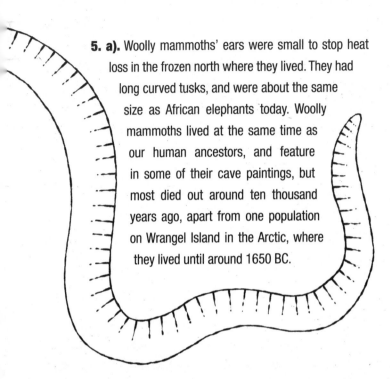

**5. a).** Woolly mammoths' ears were small to stop heat loss in the frozen north where they lived. They had long curved tusks, and were about the same size as African elephants today. Woolly mammoths lived at the same time as our human ancestors, and feature in some of their cave paintings, but most died out around ten thousand years ago, apart from one population on Wrangel Island in the Arctic, where they lived until around 1650 BC.

**6. c)** Elephant birds were probably the world's biggest birds ever – they weighed around half a tonne, and measured three metres or more tall. They were most likely wiped out because people hunted them.

**7. a).** The broad-faced potoroo has been extinct since the end of the 1800s. Like kangaroos, they were pouched animals (marsupials) with long hind legs, but were only about 25 centimetres tall. They were probably a victim of cats and dogs brought by the European settlers to Australia. Some potoroo relatives have survived in Australia.

**8. a).** There were thousands of millions of passenger pigeons in North America in the 1600s, which migrated in enormous flocks that turned the sky black. As the settlers cut down the huge forests where the pigeons lived, there began to be fewer and fewer passenger pigeons. But the birds took a real bashing from the 1800s onwards, when they were caught in nets by the tens of thousands, and eaten as a cheap source of meat. By 1914, one last passenger pigeon, called Martha, lived in Cincinnati Zoo. She died the same year.

**9. b).** The poor old gloomy tube-nosed bat has every right to be gloomy – it might even be extinct already. It's only known from one specimen, found on an island in Japan. By the way, the sad-faced woolly sloth and the murky owl-eyed lizard are made up.

**10.** All of them. Unfortunately there's a long list of animals that are in danger of extinction today – around four thousand of them, including orang-utans, various types of tiger, and less well known creatures such as the Chinese giant salamander, the purple frog and a flightless parrot called the kakapo. The main reason animals are becoming extinct today is climate change and loss of habitat (forests being cut down, or towns spreading into the countryside). In the past it was hunting (as in the case of the unfortunate but tasty passenger pigeons), so animals at risk were those that tasted nice, or had lovely fur coats, or interesting tusks or horns.

Anyway, back to the extinct dinosaurs . . . or did they really become extinct? Remember the feathers on the little *Epidexipteryx* on page 77? All today's birds are descended from a type of dinosaur, so dinosaurs do live on. Just in a far less terrifying form.

With so many big predators out of the way, mammals finally had a chance. Up to this point, they'd been pretty titchy – the biggest were only about the size of a pet cat. But things were about to change . . .

# 8
# Planet of the Apes

Soon after the dinosaurs and their friends were wiped out, a group of mammals evolved that lived in trees in the world's tropical rainforests. They probably looked a bit like squirrels and ate insects. These unassuming little creatures were about to start an evolutionary journey that would eventually reach all the way to orang-utans and bushbabies . . . and you.

Let's give them a huge cheer, because they were the world's first primates, a vital stage in making a human out of soup, and our ancestors.

## Ida and the First Primates

Although there are lots of bits and pieces scattered about in different parts of the world, there are very few complete fossils of primates. Here's the most famous one. She's been nicknamed Ida, and she's a young primate who lived around 47 million years ago.

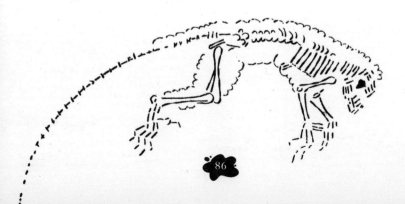

Almost all her skeleton is preserved, and even her fur has left an impression in the rock. It's amazing what you can find out from a fossil: we even know what she had for dinner because the remains of fossilised fruit and leaves were found inside her stomach. Ida had broken her wrist and, even though it had mended, it might have been why she didn't survive to become a grown-up primate – when you spend your life among the treetops, even a small problem with one of your wrists can spell disaster.

Ida's so well preserved because her body fell into the Messel Pit in Germany, a deep lake that gradually filled up with tiny bits of rock and sand and mud. The lake contained hardly any oxygen near the bottom, so scavenging bottom feeders, which might eat bodies or scatter bits of them about, couldn't survive. The perfect fossil-making conditions at the Messel Pit have created a sort of fossil zoo. An amazing variety of unfortunate animals met a gruesome end in the pit, including ancient rodents, miniature horses, giant ants, bats, and lots of different kinds of crocodile.

Ida isn't the earliest kind of primate. She was part of the group of primates that later became lemurs and lorises (super-cute little monkey-type things), tarsiers (more super-cute little monkey-types with huge eyes), monkeys and apes, including human beings. But Ida's not a direct ancestor, and her kind of primate eventually became extinct.

# What's a Primate?

Well, it's obvious, isn't it? We all look a bit like monkeys. There's a fuzzy answer to this question because primates don't have a special characteristic that no other living thing has. But they do share similar features . . .

🐾 Good vision and forward-facing eyes. Most primates have good colour vision.

🐾 Big brain compared to the size of the body. (This varies a fair bit.)

🐾 Grasping hands and feet – though humans don't have grasping feet.

🐾 Toenails – though some primates have claws on some fingers and toes.

# Some Distant Relatives

Before we meet the primates that are our closer relatives, let's say hello to some of our more distant family members who are still alive and well today. Think of them as your great-great-granddad's cousin's great-great grandchildren, who were doing their family tree and found out you're related, so they thought they'd look you up, since they were in the area.

Lemurs are only found in one place on Earth: the island of Madagascar, which is home to all sorts of creatures that are only found there, because the island became separate around 88 million years ago. An early lemur ancestor must have drifted across the sea somehow (they could have been swept out to sea by accident, floating on "rafts" of vegetation or driftwood), 40 million years ago or more. Then millions of years of evolution got to work, with some interesting results. One of them is the mouse lemur, the world's smallest primate – the titchiest kind are just nine centimetres long and weigh 30 grams, almost tiny enough to crawl up a gorilla's nostril. But even stranger is the aye-aye, another type of lemur, which looks like this:

The aye-aye comes out at night to catch its favourite food: fat grubs that live inside dead wood. It finds them by tapping on the wood, and then winkling them out, using . . . the extra-long skinny finger it's evolved for just that purpose.

Gaaah! Just look at that thing! It's unbelievably weird, and the result of evolution getting to work on an island.

# Closer Relatives

South America used to be completely isolated from North America, separated by a wide sea. Around 30 million years or so ago, primates arrived – no one knows how, maybe on a raft of floating plants. They lost no time in evolving into all sorts of different monkeys, known as New World monkeys, because South and North America were known as the New World when Europeans first got there.

New World monkeys have evolved in different ways: some of them have tails that can grasp branches to help them swing through the trees; some, the howler monkeys, have incredibly loud calls; some have bright red faces or orange beards; and some have ended up smaller than the biggest insects in South America (the titan beetle is longer than a pygmy marmoset, whose body measures just 15 centimetres).

## Second Cousins Once Removed

Meanwhile, over in Africa and Asia, about 30 million years ago primates split into two groups. One lot eventually became apes, including humans. The other lot became Old World monkeys, different from the New World monkeys over in South America, mainly because of the shape of their noses (at first, anyway).

Off went the Old World monkey and ape ancestors down their separate evolutionary paths. Try this Old World Monkey Quiz to see if you can guess how some of them ended up . . .

# MONKEY QUIZ

**1.** **What's unusual about a male mandrill's bottom?**

a) It looks almost exactly like the mandrill's face.

b) It's twice the size of the mandrill's head.

c) It's bright blue and red, like the mandrill's face.

**2.** **Female proboscis monkeys are attracted to male proboscis monkeys with . . .**

a) Thick spiky orange hair.

b) An absolutely huge nose.

c) A bright blue bottom.

**3.** **A group of Rhesus macaques in India were responsible for which of these crimes?**

a) They stole a valuable diamond.

b) They caused the death of the Deputy Mayor of Delhi.

c) They kidnapped a six-year-old child for three hours.

**4.** **What record do the Japanese macaques hold?**

a) They're the largest Old World monkeys.

b) They live the furthest north of all monkeys.

c) They're the most intelligent of all monkeys.

**5.    Which type of primate uses the most complex sounds?**

a)    Chimpanzees.

b)    Colobus monkeys.

c)    Gelada baboons.

**6.    What do monkeys have that apes don't?**

a)    Tails.

b)    Black-and-white vision.

c)    Earlobes.

**ANSWERS:**

1. c). The colours – of both ends – become especially bright when a male mandrill becomes the top monkey in his group.

2. b). The noses are ridiculously large and wobbly, and the bigger and wobblier the better, as far as female proboscis monkeys are concerned.

3. b). The unfortunate politician fell off a balcony after a group of the monkeys attacked.

4. b). Most monkeys live in tropical or subtropical parts of the world, but Japanese macaques live the furthest north, where there's thick snow in winter. Some of the monkeys sit in hot springs to warm up.

5. c). Gelada baboons are monkeys that live on grasslands in Ethiopia in groups of up to around six hundred. They make complex noises and smack their lips at the same time to communicate with one another, and the result sounds a bit like human speech.

6. a). Apes also sit or stand upright more than monkeys, and have more mobile shoulder joints.

# Apes Appear

The first apes turned up around 25 million years ago, and went on to become gibbons, known as "lesser apes", and then the "great apes". Great apes include gorillas, chimpanzees, orang-utans and people. There were other apes who died out along the way (including the biggest ape ever, which was three metres tall!), but this is how we share our family tree with the world's living apes:

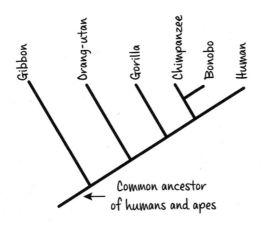

Common ancestor of humans and apes

We shared ancestors with gibbons (which are "lesser apes") until around 20 million years ago, with orang-utans until around 15 million years ago, with gorillas until around 10 million years ago, and with chimpanzees, who are our closest living relatives, until around 7 million years ago.

# Great Apes: The Essential Facts

## ORANG-UTANS

⚜ Orang-utans live only in rainforests on two islands in the
world: Borneo (part of Malaysia and Indonesia) and Sumatra
(Indonesia).

⚜ Unlike gorillas and chimps,
they're usually solitary
creatures, and unlike gorillas
and chimps they spend almost
all their time up in the trees.

⚜ Unlike just about everything
else on the planet, some males grow weird fleshy discs called
flanges around their faces – a male might suddenly grow them
even when he's been a grown-up for a while, or not grow
them at all, and no one understands why.

⚜ Orang-utans are maybe the most huggable of all the great
apes, and they have a very big hug indeed – their arm-spans
can be more than two metres long, enough to give you and
several of your friends a great big cuddle.

⚜ Although they eat mostly fruit, orang-utans have been spotted
catching and eating little primates called slow lorises.
Honestly, orang-utans, we're disappointed in you.

Logging, farming and mining in the rainforests where orang-utans live mean that these apes are losing their home at an alarming rate.

## GORILLAS

 Gorillas are the world's biggest primates and live in the forests of Central Africa.

 They can weigh up to 200 kilograms and look ferocious, but in fact they're peace-loving animals. Although . . .

 Sometimes they get a bit cross with one another, and occasionally the leader of a group of gorillas, a male silverback, can make a bit of a fuss if he feels threatened by another male gorilla, and bangs his chest, roars and throws things – nothing you don't see in the classroom on a daily basis – but no one gets hurt. Usually. OK, so occasionally there's a fight to the death.

 Gorillas are mainly vegetarian (they eat insects too sometimes) and have to eat lots of fibrous plant material to keep their massive bodies going, so they have absolutely huge jaw muscles for all that chewing, and do an awful lot of farting.

Incidentally, some scientists think that a mutant gene that led to weaker jaw muscles might have been why our ancestors developed bigger brains – there was more room for them.

## CHIMPANZEES

 Chimpanzees are the closest living relatives we've got, along with their very close relatives, bonobos (which used to be known as pygmy chimpanzees). We share more than 98 per cent of a chimp's DNA. The next time you find yourself grooming your friend for fleas and then eating them, you'll know why.

 Chimps live in groups. Big groups might number over a hundred animals.

 They eat a wide variety of food: fruit, insects and meat. Groups of chimps cooperate to hunt and kill monkeys to eat. They might scavenge meat from dead animals too.

 Chimps' use of tools is very impressive. They use sponges made from moss to soak up water, sticks to poke termite mounds to get at the termites, and stones to crack nuts.

 Chimps have been taught more than three hundred different sign language signs. In fact, some bonobos, orang-utans and gorillas have also been taught sign language successfully.

Sadly, all the great apes, our close relatives, are now endangered species, mainly because the forests where they live are being cut down.

We have plenty of even closer relatives who aren't around any more – ones who walked on two legs, like us. We'll find out about them in chapter nine.

Hang on, though. What about the rest of life on Earth . . . ?

# Other Animals

While the first primates were hopping about from branch to branch, other creatures were roaming the land and sea. For the first 20 million years or so after the dinosaurs' demise, the top predators were ferocious giant birds, or ferocious giant crocodiles, depending on whereabouts in the world you happened to be. Either way it was pretty alarming.

Around 60 million years ago, the first meat-eating mammals appeared, but they were still quite small. All sorts of things started to pop up after that: the first whales, rodents, horses and elephants. Eventually, the ancestors of today's cats and dogs – including lions and wolves, as well as our pets – got bigger and much fiercer, and became the top prey animals.

Here are some evolutionary highlights from the time of the primates . . .

# 9
# Naked Apes

After all those billions of years of slimy stuff, then millions of years of sea creatures, then the dinosaurs and mammals and primates . . . we're FINALLY getting close to making a human out of soup.

## Huggable Hominins

We share a common ancestor with our closest living relatives, chimpanzees, but we wandered off down a different evolutionary path from chimps round about 7 million years ago. Modern human beings are the only surviving member of a family of human-like animals called hominins (which is a bit confusing – it's different from hominids, which include great apes).

We've done quite well for ourselves: instead of sticking to one part of the world we've spread all over the place, developed farming and writing and clever things like that, and our use of tools is pretty impressive by anybody's standards.

Our earliest hominin ancestors were very similar to apes, probably just as hairy, and their brains were the same size, but they walked upright on two legs at least some of the time. After that came lots of different hominin species – some of them lived at the same time as one another, and some of them even met, and maybe had babies together. Some kinds died out completely, while others are our ancestors. Over time they started to look more and more like we do, and became less and less hairy.

But there's lots we don't know, and there are probably more hominins that we haven't met yet – we have to rely on things like fossils and stone tools to find out about them. The earliest hominin we've found out about so far is six million years old, and is only known because of a single skull found in Chad, in Africa. Right now, scientists are busily digging away in Africa to try to find out more.

## Home for the Holidays

Imagine it's Christmas and lots of different relatives are going to be dropping by. The difference is that these relatives have arrived by time machine. Some of them might be even odder than your Great-aunt Minty, who only eats white food and talks to her roses. So find some extra chairs and make sure there are plenty of mince pies, because it's time to meet the family . . .

# GREAT-GREAT-AUNT ARDI

*Ardipithecus ramidus* – the scientists who discovered her nicknamed her Ardi, so let's call her that as well – lived around 4.5 million years ago. Like the rest of your ancient relatives, you won't get much out of her in the way of conversation, but do offer her a bowl of fruit and nuts. (She might eat insects and small mammals as well, but let's stick to a vegetarian diet to be on the safe side.) She walks on two legs for at least some of the time, but a climbing frame would make a good Christmas present because Ardi has evolved to grasp branches with her hands and feet, and might feel out of place in an armchair and start climbing the curtains.

Ardi is the oldest hominin skeleton that's ever been found – so far. There are bits and pieces of older hominins, though, like the six-million-year-old skull found in Chad on page 101.

## GREAT-AUNT LUCY

Great-aunt Lucy is a member of a species called *Australopithecus afarensis*, who lived from around 3.7 to 3 million years ago. Her name doesn't mean she comes from Australia – it means "Southern ape from Afar", which is a region in Ethiopia (all of these early hominins come from Africa). There's some evidence to suggest that Lucy used stone tools, though it's far from certain, but give her some cutlery just in case (you wouldn't want to insult her).

A fair bit of a female skeleton from Lucy's species was discovered in 1974, the most complete hominin skeleton found up until that time, and scientists called it Lucy after a song they were listening to while they celebrated their discovery, "Lucy in the Sky with Diamonds" by The Beatles.

## UNCLE EREC

Uncle Erec looks very similar to us modern humans, but conversation will still be difficult (he might sound a bit grunty), and you might be better off with sign language. Uncle Erec, a member of the species

*Homo erectus*, lived from 1.8 million years ago to 200,000 years ago, or even more recently than that, and was probably the first hominin to leave Africa. He looks a lot like we do, and isn't anywhere near as hairy as the first hominins. His species has also been found in China, Indonesia, Africa and Europe, though scientists argue about whether the remains found in Africa and Europe are slightly different species. Uncle Erec was probably the first hominin to use fire and hand axes.

Uncle Erec wasn't the first hominin to use tools, though – that was an earlier species, *Homo habilis*.

 ## QUICK QUIZ QUESTION

**A new species of hominin, *Homo floresiensis*, was discovered in 2003. What's its nickname?**

a)   Humphry

b)   The Hobbit

c)   Hagrid

d)   Jar Jar Binks

**ANSWER:**

b). Fossils of the new species were found on the island of Flores in Indonesia. These hominins were very small (not much more than a metre tall) with small brains, but used fire and stone tools and hunted animals. They lived on the island from about 92,000 years ago until 12,000 years ago – just the other day, really. They're the most recent hominin to become extinct, though they're not the closest relative of modern humans.

# AUNTY HEIDI

Aunty Heidi will feel most at home in your living room, because her species, *Homo heidelbergensis*, was probably the first to build shelters. Heidi might be a descendant of Uncle Erec, and her species lived from southern Africa all the way to Europe, 600,000 to 250,000 years ago. She might even have been around at the same time as the first modern humans. But Aunty Heidi is definitely a very close relative – so you might find that you have lots in common.

There are more hominin species that we know about – in fact altogether there are more than twenty that we've found out about because of fossils – but we'd never fit them all into your living room.

# Meet the Neanderthals

Two new types of hominin turned up from around 350,000 years ago, both of them the descendants of Aunty Heidi and her kind. The first to appear were the Neanderthals. They evolved from some of the more enterprising and intrepid of Aunty Heidi's species, who'd left Africa and travelled to Europe. They're our closest relatives, so we should definitely say hello.

They were shorter and stockier and had paler skin and hair than other hominins who were around at the time, so they were better suited to a colder, less sunny European climate. Neanderthals' brains were just as big as ours (and in some cases bigger), and their noses were much bigger (maybe best not to mention that though, they're probably a bit sensitive about them). Like modern humans they wore clothes and jewellery, used stone tools, hunted, made fires, looked after old and sick people, buried their dead and made art. They sound absolutely lovely, don't they?

### ?? QUICK QUIZ QUESTION ??

**Who were the Denisovians?**

a) Another type of hominin who lived at the same time as the Neanderthals.

b) Modern humans who lived in Denisovia in Mongolia.

c) A group of Neanderthals who made elaborate cave paintings.

d) Visitors from the planet Denisovia who shared their technology with Neanderthals.

The first Neanderthal fossil was discovered in the Neander Valley (which is how they got their name), Germany, in 1856. It was the first fossil to be identified as an extinct type of human, and you can imagine how some of the Victorians reacted to that.

Neanderthals died out around 28,000 years ago, but not before they'd met another type of hominin . . .

# Meanwhile, Over in Africa . . .

It's time for a really long, dramatic drum roll and a huge fanfare, because, at last . . .

# HUMANS EVOLVED!

Yes! It's the moment we've all been waiting for – for billions of years, actually. Modern human beings like us, *Homo sapiens*, evolved in Africa around 200,000 years ago. That deserves a standing ovation at the very least.

## On the Move

You know how it is: you get comfortable, and you just can't be bothered to move. We humans were happy to stay where we were, in Africa, for the first 100,000 years or so. By that time some of us had got a bit bored, and started to spread out, to the Middle East, southern and South Asia, and Australia.

A few tens of thousands of years after that, we were off again – north into Europe. When we got there we were in for a big surprise: the Neanderthals, who were already there. In fact,

Neanderthals and their ancestors had already been there for hundreds of thousands of years.

What do you think happened? Did we fight the Neanderthals, or make friends and live happily ever after?

It was a long time ago, and no one was keeping records or writing things down, so we don't really know what happened. But the Neanderthals definitely died out after we modern humans had been in Europe for a few thousand years. You have to admit, that looks a bit suspicious. On the other hand, we also know that some modern humans and Neanderthals did make friends. In fact some of them went a bit further than that – they had children together.

We know this because some of us share DNA with Neanderthals – people from Europe, Asia and New Guinea have a little bit of Neanderthal in them. So Neanderthals still walk the earth – and maybe someone you know inherited their big nose from a distant Neanderthal ancestor (again, though, it might be best not to point this out).

After we'd had a good look round Europe, taking in the sights and setting up home in caves, some of us continued north all the way to Siberia, where we had to contend with very cold temperatures but met helpful woolly mammoths. They were helpful because we ate them, used their fur to keep warm, and even built huts from their bones.

We eventually arrived in North and South America, and as far as we know, no other earlier species of human ever made it there. The last places on Earth we got to were the islands of the South Pacific: to reach them, we had to cross 30,000 square kilometres of uncharted Pacific Ocean, with absolutely no idea what was on the other side, in fairly small boats, with only the stars to help us navigate. But somehow, we managed it. Modern humans set out from New Guinea around three thousand years ago, and by about a thousand years ago people had spread all the way to Hawaii, the Cook Islands, Easter Island and New Zealand.

HUMANS HAD TAKEN OVER THE WORLD!

# 10

# The Rest is History

Once modern humans had turned up, and travelled all over the planet, we started to leave lots more clues behind about ourselves and what we were up to. Eventually, about five thousand years ago, we started writing things down. The world wasn't prehistoric any more, because written history had begun.

In the last twelve thousand years, humans changed from hunting and gathering to farming, which meant we could stay in one place, and sometimes produce more food than we needed, so we could grow in numbers and our villages could grow in size. Soon the first cities appeared, and the first countries and empires, and before you knew it someone had invented the wheel and everyone was having an industrial revolution and driving cars and things. And not long after that we were leaving planet Earth altogether and taking trips into space.

As a human being, you might well feel pretty pleased with yourself. Look at all the stuff humans have achieved – smartphones and space stations and the Internet, and organ transplants and antibiotics and vaccines against disease. On the other hand, we do have a habit of fighting wars with one another, and we're rubbish at sharing things out equally to make sure no one ends up hungry or with nowhere to live. As well as being kind and caring and generally very nice, human beings can also be cruel and selfish and generally pretty horrible.

## A Final Thought

And finally . . . what's going to happen in the future? Might we grow wings or something epic like that at some stage?

**? ? ?**

Well . . . probably not. The last time we were in danger of evolving wings was 50 million years ago, when bats first took off.

The human race might be affected artificially, though, as we find out more about genetics, and can select features for babies before they're born. Or maybe we'll end up having bits of electronics inside us to make us run, think and learn faster – or even immediately . . . just imagine, there could one day be a world without times tables.

At this very moment, people are searching for planets a bit like Earth, so that one day we might go off in a spaceship and live there. If we carry on ruining our own planet, or if there are too many of us, we might have to. If that happens in the future, we might need to change to suit ourselves to the new conditions – maybe the gravity will be different, or the gases in the atmosphere.

In the meantime, though, before you embark on any interplanetary voyages, go and have a look at yourself in the mirror. Your species has evolved over thousands of millions of years, from a self-copying molecule, to a fishy thing with legs, to something that looked very similar to a dinosaur, to an insect-eating rat . . . all the way to the complicated, clever and – it has to be said – drop-dead gorgeous creature you see in the mirror.

You've survived hundreds of metres of thick ice, volcanic eruptions, fearsome predators and asteroid hits. It's a real piece of luck that you're here at all. You – and the spiders, kangaroos, oak trees, coelacanths and everything else on earth – are amazing.

# TIMELINE

Us human beings have only appeared on the face of the Earth very recently indeed. Think of the formation of planet Earth as the bottom of the Eiffel Tower. Life begins about a quarter of the way up, then nothing apart from single-celled organisms appear until three-quarters of the way to the top. Exciting things like dinosaurs don't turn up until the antenna on the very top, and human beings only arrive right on that last little nobbly bit on the top of that. (Roughly.)

| | |
|---|---|
| **4600 mya (million years ago)** | Planet Earth forms. |
| **3600 mya** | The first simple cells evolve. |
| **3400 mya** | The Earth is covered in bluey-green slimy stuff (cyanobacteria), and stays that way for another 1,400 million years. |
| **2000 mya** | More complex cells, called protists, evolve. |
| **1600 mya** | Protists evolve that have lots of cells. |
| **750–580 mya** | Period of Snowball Earth, when the planet is covered in thick ice. |

| | |
|---|---|
| **600 mya** | The first simple animals evolve. |
| **570–510 mya** | Cambrian period, when lots of new life evolves. |
| **535 mya** | The first fish put in an appearance. |
| **488 mya** | The Great Ordovician Biodiversification Event. |
| **450 mya** | The first land plants and fungi. |
| **440 mya** | Mass extinction. |
| **360 mya** | Tetrapods (our earliest ancestors who lived on land) crawl out of the seas and oceans. |
| **359 mya** | Another mass extinction. |
| **300 mya** | The Earth's continents are joined together in a supercontinent known as Pangaea. |
| **250 mya** | The End Permian mass extinction when 95 per cent of everything dies out. |
| **230 mya** | The first dinosaurs walk the Earth. |

| 200 mya | Another mass extinction – a relatively minor one this time. |
|---|---|
| 200 mya | The first mammals evolve (there's a lot of argument about when this was). |
| 130 mya | The first flowering plants pop up. |
| 65 mya | Yet another mass extinction. The dinosaurs – and lots of other things – die out. |
| 65 mya | The first primates start swinging from the trees. |
| 60 mya | The first meat-eating mammals start gnawing on gristly things. |
| 35 mya | Lots of modern groups of mammals appear. |
| 25 mya | The first apes turn up. |
| 20 mya | India crashes into Asia and creates the Himalayas. |
| 6 mya | Our earliest hominin ancestors evolve. |

| | |
|---|---|
| **1.8 mya** | *Homo erectus* turns up, and sticks around until around 200,000 years ago. |
| **600,000 years ago** | *Homo heidelbergensis* arrived, the ancestors of both Neanderthals and modern humans. |
| **500,000 years ago** | By around this time our human-like ancestors could control fire. |
| **350,000 years ago** | The first Neanderthals turn up in Europe. |
| **200,000 years ago** | The first modern humans evolve in Africa. |
| **100,000 years ago** | Some modern humans get itchy feet and start to leave Africa and spread out around the world. |
| **77,000 years ago** | The first known human artwork is engraved onto a piece of red ochre in a cave in South Africa. |
| **75,000 years ago** | People are wearing jewellery by around this time. |
| **35,000 years ago** | The world's first musical instruments that we know about are made – flutes made from bone. |

| | |
|---|---|
| **28,000 years ago** | The Neanderthals die out. |
| **6500 years ago** | Uruk, probably the world's first city, grows up around this time (in modern-day Iraq). |
| **5000 years ago** | Writing is invented in ancient Sumer (modern-day Iraq). The first wheels (that we know about) start rolling around the same time. |
| **1822** | Gregor Mendel is born – he went on to discover how different features are inherited. |
| **1858** | Darwin and Wallace's scientific paper on natural selection is published. |
| **1953** | Watson and Crick publish their discovery of the structure of DNA. |
| **1961** | Yuri Gagarin becomes the first human being in space. |

# Tricky Words

Here's a reminder of what some of the scientific or difficult words in this book mean. A few of them aren't in this book at all, but we've put them in because we like them. Also because you might come across them if you're reading other books about evolution.

**Amino acid:** one of more than fifty molecules used inside the body to build proteins.

**Anthropoid:** "higher primates", or monkeys and apes (including us) are called anthropoids – a different group from the "lower primates" – tarsiers, lemurs, lorises, etc.

**Arthropod:** group that includes insects, spiders, crabs and lobsters – animals without a backbone but with an external skeleton.

**Atom:** tiny building blocks that make up everything in the universe.

**Australopithicene:** an early type of human that lived in Africa.

**Bacteria:**    microscopic single-celled organisms.

**Billion:**    a thousand million.

**Cell:**    tiny structure that makes up living things.

**Chromosome:**    a structure inside the nucleus of a cell containing DNA.

**Common ancestor:**    the most recent species from which two or more other species evolved.

**Continental drift:**    the gradual movement of the continents on Earth as the plates that make up the Earth's crust move. German scientist Alfred Wegener came up with the idea in 1912.

**DNA:**    short for deoxyribonucleic acid, a molecule found in the cells of all living things that contains genetic information in a chemical code.

**Embryo:**    group of cells that develops into a baby living thing.

**Enzyme:**    complex proteins inside cells that cause particular reactions.

**Evolution:** the process of change in living things over time that happens because of natural selection.

**Fossil:** remains of ancient animals and plants.

**Gene:** a section of code in DNA that makes a particular reaction inside a cell.

**Genetic drift:** random changes in a population's genes.

**Genetics:** the study of genes and the effects of genes.

**Genome:** the complete genetic information for a living thing.

**Hominid:** the group that includes great apes and humans.

**Hominin:** humans and their human-like ancestors after the split from the last common ancestor of humans and chimpanzees.

**Hybrid:** offspring of two parents each from a different species.

**Invertebrate:** an animal without a backbone.

**Mammal**: animals that have backbones, hair and feed milk to their young.

**Mesozoic**: the age of the dinosaurs, which is split into the Triassic, Jurassic and Cretaceous.

**Molecule**: two or more atoms that form a chemical bond with one another.

**Mutation**: a change to a gene that has an effect (which can be helpful, harmful or neutral) on the living thing.

**Natural selection**: the process that causes evolution – individuals with the most suitable features are more likely to survive and pass on their features.

**New World**: North and South America.

**Old World**: Europe, Asia and Africa.

**Organism**: living thing.

**Prehistoric**: before written history.

**Primate:** group of mammals including apes (and humans) and monkeys.

**Primordial soup:** the mix of chemicals on Earth when it first formed. Soviet biologist Alexander Oparin first described early Earth conditions as "primordial soup" in 1924.

**Protein:** complex molecules made of amino acids that have an essential role inside the body.

**Pterosaur:** extinct flying reptile.

**RNA:** ribonucleic acid, a self-copying molecule.

**Sex chromosome:** pair of chromosomes, either XX or XY, which determines whether a baby is male or female.

**Trilobite:** extinct sea-living arthropod.

**Trillion:** a million times a million.

**Vertebrate:** an animal with a backbone.

# About the Author

**Tracey Turner** has written more than fifty books
for children on a variety of subjects, from rude words
to the entire history of the universe. Her books include
the bestselling *101 Things You Need to Know* and
the acclaimed Comic Strip series. She lives in Bath
with Tom and their son Toby.

# About the Illustrator

Artist and author **Sally Kindberg** has a vast experience of working on books and features, and running drawing workshops for both children and adults in venues as far apart as China and Shetland. Sally recently drew the Comic Strip History of Space. Her current book series is Draw It!, encouraging children to draw things they have never thought of drawing before.